Author profile http://www.ebooksbydarren.com

I0503378

Blog http://www.darrenackers.com/

Twitter https://twitter.com/darren_ackers

LinkedIn https://uk.linkedin.com/in/darrenackers

Disclaimer and FTC Compliance

This book is for the sole purpose of entertainment. All the views detailed in this book are those of the author, therefore should not be taken as any from of instruction of an expert. The reader is solely responsible for their actions.

Both the author and the publisher does not accept any responsibility or liability whatsoever on behalf of the purchaser or reader of these materials.

As an affiliate marketer my eBooks on occasions contain affiliate links - simply put, I will receive a commission payment on a purchase through the affiliate link. I advise you to carry out your own research before completing a purchase. All affiliate products I promote in my eBooks are products that I have personally used and have found to be useful.

My Free Gift to You

Thank you for purchasing my book. I would like to offer you this Free Gift - my Twitter Marketing eBook. In this free book I will share you with what I've learnt to market my online and offline businesses.

This eBook contains over 5,000 words.

In this book I will share:

Building Your List of Followers

Why Re-Tweeting Helps

Tools for Easier and Wiser Twittering

Tools to Send Friendly Auto DM's

Turning Your Followers into Your Customers

How to Maximize Your Traffic on Twitter

Usual Mistakes Committed by Twitter Users

Additional Tips in Twitter Marketing

Here's the download link.

http://www.darrenackers.com/free-twitter-marketing-guide

Introduction

For many years I have been fortunate enough to earn a secondary passive income promoting Clickbank products as an affiliate marketer. I wrote this book to share what I've learnt promoting Clickbank products. This book is for the beginner, intermediate, and if you are an experienced Clickbank affiliate marketer, then you may derive some benefit from my marketing methods and how to effectively track profitable keywords and phrases.

When I began promoting Clickbank products, there were no blueprints or tutorials available to set me on the right path, therefore I had no choice but to learn the hard way. When I finally grasped how to find a profitable Clickbank product and how to market a Clickbank product, I never looked back. Once I understood Clickbank and developed an effective marketing strategy, month after month I have earned a secondary income as a Clickbank affiliate.

Table of Contents

Tracking Your Performing Keyword and Phrases

Bevo Media Affiliate Tracking

Six Methods to Promote a Clickbank Product

What is Clickbank

I'm assuming that you're a Clickbank newbie when I say....Clickbank is a market place where vendors meet affiliates. A vendor is a product owner; someone who develops Clickbank products. The products which they create are typically are how to eBooks, software training programs and video courses. An affiliate is the person who promotes the vendors products and in return earns a commission when he or she makes a sale.

The majority of affiliate marketers that I know rank Clickbank as their number one place to source and promote digital products. Of all the affiliate networks I have tested, by far, Clickbank is the easiest to navigate and they pay the highest commission. Affiliates like me trust Clickbank, because Clickbank pays commission payments by weekly direct bank transfer. Furthermore, their tracking and reporting is first class. Their back office applications are designed to provide flexible ways to track affiliate sales and click throughs. Click throughs are when a website visitor clicks on an affiliate link and is directed to the vendors sales page. All this will be explained in a later chapter.

What a Clickbank Newbie Needs to Know

There are many affiliates who earn six-figure and seven-figure incomes selling Clickbank products. The earning potential for newbie affiliate marketers is very attractive because you can easily make two sales per day after a few months promoting Clickbank products. For example, following the successful selection of a profitable product, a newbie making two sales per day could earn over one thousand dollars per month.

The typical commission paid on a Clickbank sale is 70% and the average sale is forty five dollars. Based on a 70% commission, the affiliate will earn approximately thirty dollars per sale. Two sales per day equates to eighteen hundred dollars per month and twenty one thousand dollars per year.

So you can see how the money soon racks up. The trick to earning money online is to create a marketing strategy to sell products and then scale this up and rinse and repeat.

At the end of this book I have detailed a blueprint which I use to promote Clickbank products to earn a secondary income.

The strategy which I've developed only requires me to work a few hours each week to maintain this secondary income.

When do You Get Paid

Before you receive your first commission payout from Clickbank, you need to make five product sales. Clickbank's customer distribution requirement, CDR, requires an affiliate to make five sales and the buyers who bought the products must pay using at least two of the following payment methods: American Express, Carte Bleue, Diners Card, Discover, European Direct Debit, JCB, Maestro, MasterCard, PayPal, and Visa. Clickbank puts this requirement in place to prevent affiliates fraudulently collecting rebates on their purchase.

My advice is to never purchase a product using your affiliate account until you have made the five sales and complied with their CDR policy. Until five sales have been made, Clickbank will pay affiliates by check. After you have made a few sales, you can set your payment to be paid by direct bank transfer.

However Clickbank only pays by direct bank transfer to certain countries. Furthermore, when you first set up your account, I strongly suggest that you set your payment threshold to ten dollars. The default setting is one hundred dollars. To change your payment threshold to ten dollars, simply click the settings tab, click edit, and then select payment threshold. This is found to the right of payment information.

Understanding the Clickbank Marketplace

When you login on the Clickbank website, click on Marketplace. The menu down the left will look confusing. Let me explain since understanding the terminology in this paragraph will help you to find a hot selling Clickbank product in little time.

There are two ways to search for a product. You can use the advance search bar, perform a keyword search, or browse the categories on the left. At last count, there were twenty three main categories with a variety of subcategories listed under each main category.

The keyword search uses a Boolean method which allows you to search using "and" to combine words, and "not" to exclude words. By placing a keyword or keyword phrase in quotes, you get an exact match and the displayed products will be aligned to your search.

Now to explain the jargon terms on the left menu.

Initial Sale: This means the commission that the average affiliate earns. This includes upsells and refunds.

Average Rebill Total: This applies to subscription products such as a membership site where the customer pays a monthly fee to access the products.

Average Sale: This figure is the average commission based on the initial sale plus any recurring billing. Recurring billing applies to subscription products.

Average Percent Sale: This figure is the average commission on the initial sale, upsells, and recurrent sales.

Average Percent Rebill: This figure is only shown if the vendor offers recurring billing products.

Grav: This is the main figure that I use. Grav means gravity. This is a calculation to show how often the product is sold by affiliates in a 12 week period. The hottest Clickbank product has the highest gravity rating.

Cat: This is where you see the categories and subcategories.

You will also see these terms are associated with icons. An icon to look out for is the spanner and screwdriver icon. This icon means that the vendor has affiliate tools on their website. Affiliate tools are a sign of authority and the vendor has taken the time to help the affiliate with their marketing. I will cover this more in the strategy section.

Understanding Clickbank Reporting

To be successful as a Clickbank affiliate, you need to understand Clickbank's Reporting and Clickbank's TID. The TID is the tracking ID which is appended to the generated affiliate link.

Here is an explanation of the top bar phrases which you need to know. On the home affiliates page, click on Reporting and then click Analytics. This page is the main reporting page where you can see specific details regarding the products you are promoting. This screen allows you to view data such as date range, initial sales, refunds, and charge backs. You can also sort the data by hops. A hop is a click through which is when a visitor clicks on the affiliate link and is redirected to the vendors sales page.

I have found that Clickbank reporting is accurate since all their reporting data excludes search engine bots. A search engine using bots to crawl the internet and they crawl affiliate links. Therefore if Clickbank counted bots in their reporting, the data would be inaccurate because the bot is not a prospective buyer.

Sorting the Data to Analyze the Tacking ID's

On the Reporting/ Analytics page you will see the 'HOPS' menu located on the left side. The full menu looks like this:

- By Vendor
- By Tracking Id
- By Customer Country

Now if you click on 'Tracking ID' you will see the 'Hops by Tracking ID' page. Clickbank reporting as a whole can be confusing. I have found that the data displayed on the 'Hops by Tracking ID' page is sufficient to track your affiliate efforts. To keep the reporting simple, here's a list of the columns which I focus on:

Tracking ID: This displays all the TID's you created. For example, say you publish a YouTube video advertising the Clickbank product, the TID you create could be YouTube. So if a sale occurs from your YouTube video, your YouTube TID will be listed under the Tracking ID column.

Hop count: This is the number of the click throughs to the vendors page.

Earnings per hop: The number of hops that you need to earn your specified amount.

Hops per order: This is a guide to illustrate how many hops you need to make a sale.

Sales amount: Your total commission earned, including any refunds.

Now obviously there are more columns. However, these are the main columns that I use. By using the above columns, you get to know the important data such as number click throughs, the conversion rate, the number of product click throughs and how much you get paid.

By knowing this information, you will be able to make tweaks on how you market the Clickbank products, and discover which marketing strategies are the most effective. By knowing which marketing strategies work best, you can then rinse and repeat to make more sales.

All successful affiliate marketers' constantly track their marketing campaigns. Later in this book, I will introduce you to Bevo Media which is a great online tracking system.

More on Clickbank's Gravity

As previously mentioned, the gravity number is the most important figure to focus on. The gravity calculation displays the best selling products on Clickbank. Personally, my preference is to select a product that has a gravity above 50. The gravity calculation is an algorithm exclusive to Clickbank. The calculation is the number of affiliates who have sold a product in a 12 week period.

For many years products in the relationship, make money, and weight loss niches tend to be the best sellers and have the highest gravity score. Furthermore, products with the highest gravity are also in the most competitive niches. Some affiliates tend to be hesitant to promote products in a complex niche.

My preference has always been to promote products in a competitive niche. For me a competitive niche is proof that there is a hungry market and buyers are willing to spend money purchasing products to solve their problems.

To be a successful affiliate, you need to have an interest in any niche that you operate in. Without interest you will get bored and you will lose your focus. Losing focus is a sure way to fail and make zero money online. The ideal scenario is to operate in a niche where you have knowledge and therefore marketing the products will be easier and enjoyable.

How to Build Your Clickbank Affiliate Link and Add a TID

Once you have chosen your product, you need to create your affiliate link and TID. To do this, click on Promote, and the link builder will pop up. You will see two fields – Nickname and Tracking ID. The nickname field should display your affiliate username. If it doesn't, type it in. The tracking ID is where you type your unique TID. A TID is the unique text to track the click throughs and sales. To recap, the TID is used in the analytics section so you can track and analyze your marketing campaigns.

Let's take a YouTube campaign as an example. One marketing strategy is recording product reviews recommending a Clickbank product. Your YouTube video could be recommending a fat loss Clickbank product and your TID could 'youtube.ft1'. If this YouTube video results in a sale, this TID 'youtube.ft1' will be displayed on the Analytics page which we discussed earlier.

Like I said, to be a successful internet marketer you must track all results. In addition, you must make a note of each TID you create. The best way to keep track and record your TID's is using an Excel spreadsheet.

To record this information, I create 5 columns in an Excel spreadsheet. The titles for each column are; Product Name, Affiliate Link, TID, Where The TID Is Advertised and Notes. I use the Notes columns to record specific detail about the marketing strategy. For example, if the marketing strategy involved a video, I will detail if the video involved a PowerPoint presentation or involved speaking directly into the camera.

Try Out the Product Before You Review It

Before you promote a Clickbank product, it's a good idea to either buy the product or ask the vendor for free copy. Once you have tested or read the product, you can then write or record an accurate review. I personally prefer to have tested the product since it will help me to write a thorough review and will result in more sales.

Before purchasing the product ask the vendor for a copy to review. The majority of Clickbank vendors will oblige and send you a copy of their product at no cost. To increase your chance and receive a free copy, you need to demonstrate that you are a serious internet marketer.

To convince the vendor, I write a review of their product on my blog, and record a YouTube video about their product. These two methods in tandem convince the vendor. If the vendor refuses to send you a free copy, then purchase the product. It's common for an affiliate to purchase the product using their affiliate link. By doing this, they will earn commission and will reduce the overall price they pay for a product. If you buy the product using your affiliate link, please do not then request a refund. Any refund will affect your future commission payments, because Clickbank will make financial deductions. They will think that you are promoting products incorrectly and will penalize you.

Vendors Affiliate Tools

To help you create product reviews, successful vendors will have affiliate tools on their website. Affiliate tools are images, review articles, articles, and autoresponder messages. Affiliate tools are designed to help an affiliate sell the vendors product.

If the vendor has an affiliate tools section, I recommend that you take advantage and use them. A successful vendor will have researched their niche before they create their product and their affiliate tools. My advice is to contact the vendor and ask them questions. A typical question I ask is which problem they feel that their product solves. Another question I ask is which keywords I should use to promote their product.

You might think that keywords and the problems are obvious; however, there is no harm in asking the vendor to ascertain their views. Remember, they have carried out the research and they will most probably keep tweaking their sales page and keep discovering exactly which problems are best to focus on.

Always focus on problems and benefits. I have always found that reviewing products is the best way to sell Clickbank products. The key to a review is to focus on the prospective buyers' problem and then exaggerate the problem by explaining the further problems that can happen. By talking about problems, the prospective buyer will realize that you understand their problems and issues. Always try to tap into their emotions by using words like *sad, lonely, insecure, rejecting, embarrassed, trust, nervous, frustrated, neglected, scared, disappointed, depressed, relieve, bored, safe, etc.*

I always write in a way that lets the prospective buyer know what they are feeling and the negative impacts that their problem has on their life. Then, when talking or selling the product benefits, I talk about how the product can have a positive impact on their lives. The majority of the time you will see an example of this on the vendors sales page. The sentences are displayed as bullet points and testimonials describe how the person solved their problem with the product.

When talking of benefits, you need to put yourself in the buyer's mind and help them visualize how this product will solve their problem. When someone buys a product online, the majority of the time people like to search for a review for reassurance. It's human nature that we need reassurance before we pull out our wallets and buy a product. The same applies to selling Clickbank products. From experience, the best product reviews that produce sales are reviews which engage with the reader and are not too sales focused.

CB Analytics

CB Analytics, known as Clickbank Analytics, is an alternative site to source Clickbank products. It's an alternative to the Clickbank marketplace. CB Analytics simplifies searching through dozens of products in the Clickbank marketplace. The site is dedicated to keeping affiliates up-to-date with new products, trends and analytics. The only negative point about CB Analytics is you still need to visit the Clickbank marketplace to create your affiliate link.

CB Analytics New Product RSS

A unique feature of CB Analytics is the RSS subscription to find new products. As an affiliate marketer, it's a good idea to be kept up-to-date with the latest Clickbank products. By signing up to their RSS feed, you can be kept up-to-date automatically using an RSS reader like Google's FeedBurner. Use this link to visit CB analytics new page product page http://www.cb-analytics.com/new-products.php. Furthermore, you could bookmark this page and visit it on a regular basis to see the latest products on Clickbank.

How to Get Notified Instantly of a Clickbank Sale

Do you have a Wordpress blog? If you do, that's great because there's a plugin called 'Clickbank Notification Sale' which immediately informs you by email when you make a Clickbank sale. The plugin is getting quite old now and doesn't appear to have been updated for some time, but it still works. You can install the plugin by searching for it in the *add new plugin section* of your Wordpress site or go here and download the plugin https://wordpress.org/plugins/clickbank-sale-notification/.

Here's how to set up the plugin.

- Install Clickbank Sale Notification plugin and register with your name and email.

- Next you need to get a Clickbank Secret Key. To get this you login to your Clickbank.com account and click on Settings and the My Sites.

- Click on Edit, next to Advanced Tools, and create a Secret Key using up to 16 characters/digits. They must be all in Capital Letters and no more than 16 characters and digits.

- In the Instant Notification URL box, enter http://www.yourdomain/notify.php and select version Pin 6.0 and click Test IPN. Make sure it changes to Verified.

- Now go back to the admin back office of your Wordpress and under Settings, click Clickbank Sale Notification and add the Secret Key you created and add your email address.

That's it. Now when you make a Clickbank sale, you will receive instant notification by email. You will also be notified of any refunds.

How to Find Profitable Keywords

Knowing which keywords and phrases prospective buyers search for is crucial in affiliate marketing. Using the correct keywords to promote a product is imperative when making money online.

If you fail to use these keywords and phrases, your marketing efforts will be a waste of time. A simple way to find profitable keywords and phrases is using Traffic Travis. Traffic Travis uses Google Adwords to source the most popular keywords searched online. Here is more information on Traffic Travis.

Traffic Travis is a really cool piece of software and the best part it's free. In saying that, they also offer a paid PRO version with additional functionality, but the free version does the job nicely for keyword research. Click here to sign up for your free copy http://www.traffictravis.com. I must confess that I use the PRO version, but for keyword research the free version is suitable.

The free version offers many features for websites such as Page Rank, Backlink Checker, SEO Page Warnings and PPC

Keyword Research. Before you start using Traffic Travis you need to set up a free Google Adwords account. If you don't have one, do not worry as you can set this up through Traffic Travis. To add your Adwords account details, simply click on the File menu which is located on the top menu bar.

For the purpose of finding keywords and phrases, all you need to use is the Research function. Type a few words into the Keyword field that are associated with your niche and then Traffic Travis will search and display related keywords. Next to each keyword you will see a number which relates to the number of average global monthly searches on Google for that keyword. My recommendation is only use keywords with 1,000 plus exact global searches. To search for exact, you need to click on Advanced Settings.

Set up a Wordpress Blog

Wordpress is the most popular software used to set up a blog. A Wordpress blog is the perfect website to sell Clickbank products because it's a free open source application and there are many developers who develop free plugins which are used to customize a Wordpress site.

The mistake many people make is to create a blog on a free hosted blogging platform such as Wordpress.com and Blogspot.com. These free blogging platforms are hosted, which means your blog is hosted on their servers and they own your blog. So, if I used a free hosted platform to host my blog, my domain name would look like www.darenstock.wordpress.com.

Why you shouldn't use hosted blogging platforms

First off, these free hosted blogging platforms can take your site down at any time. They control your site and they can delete your site at the click of a button. In addition these free hosted platforms restrict the customization, so you can't use most of the free open source plugins.

Please take my advice; if you are serious about making money online please don't take an easy route, and use a free hosted blogging platform. My advice is always to buy a domain name, and pay for web hosting. The cost to purchase a domain name and a web hosting account is between 60 to 100 dollars per year.

There are many web hosting companies to choose from. My advice is to use a US based web hosting company. A web hosting company which I recommend is Bluehost.com, click here to visit http://www.bluehost.com. I have been using Bluehost for many years. For a small fee, I can host an unlimited number of Wordpress blogs. Bluehost uses the cPanel which is an easy to navigate control panel used to control a web hosting account.

cPanel allows me to create unlimited email addresses, unlimited Wordpress blogs and offers a range of additional useful features.

Furthermore Bluehosts 24x7 support is first class; whenever I experience a technical problem their support teams have always fixed this technical problem within a few hours.

Set Up a Review Page on Your Blog

One of the best ways to promote a Clickbank product is to create a review page. Review pages are by far the best method to convert at visitor into a buyer. Your job as an affiliate marketer is to introduce a product which solves the visitor's problem. By writing a well constructed review with features and benefits, you will get a visitor curious and encourage them to click through to the vendor sales page. Your role as an affiliate marketer is to subtly pre sell the product and direct the visitor to the vendors sales page. The vendors job is to hard sell and close the sale using their sales page.

Build a List and Make Money for a Long Time to Come

If you are serious in building an affiliate marketing business, you have to build a subscriber email list. A subscriber email list is where you encourage people to sign up for your newsletter or download a free product in return for their email address.

The majority of successful affiliate marketers have the opinion that sending a visitor straight to the product offer is a waste of time. When you send a new visitor straight to the product offer, you only have one chance in making a sale. By building an email list, you can keep sending your subscribers' product offers forever. Now, obviously these subscribers need to remain on your list and not unsubscribe.

To build an email list you need to create a landing page commonly known as a squeeze page. A well constructed squeeze page will encourage a visitor to sign up for your free product in exchange for their email address. In addition, you need to give the visitor two choices; sign up for your free gift or click and leave your site.

When I create a squeeze page on my blog, I always remove the sidebars and menus. By removing the sidebars and menus, the visitor cannot click and visit another page on your blog. This prevents them from getting distracted by reading any further articles on your site. Removing these distractions will result in more visitors signing up for your free product.

My advice is to focus on 5 key elements when building a squeeze page which are:

Talk to your audience

Think of the person who you want to download your free gift. Make sure your gift is what the person is looking for and is aligned with their problem. For example, if your website is about relationships, offering a free product on building a shed is a waste of time. This person wants a product to solve their relationship problem.

A sleek and attractive design

You need a clutter-free page with high resolution images. Use phrases to describe what they will learn. Use phrases which describe what's in it for them. In addition, use bright colors and create a design that is easy on the eye when using a small monitor or mobile device.

A bold headline to grab their attention

Your headline should explain what the free products is, and how it will help them. Ask yourself 'Would I download this free gift?'

A free gift

Your free gift needs to be a quality product. Typical free gifts include video courses eBooks or PDF reports, whichever product you choose please ensure its high quality. If you decide on an eBook or PDF report, ensure it is well written and produces value to the subscriber.

A simple signup form

You need to make it easy for the visitor to sign up and receive their free gift. Only ask for their first name and email address. Place a call to action below or above the sign up form. A call to action tells the visitors what they should do next. A call to action could be 'sign up today and receive your free gift in seconds'. A tip which I have learned over the years is not sending too many sales and promotional emails on a regular basis.

Your focus should be to engage your subscribers and build deep relationships with them. Building a relationship with the subscriber will result in lower unsubscribes and will keep subscribers on your list for a longer period of time. To prevent them from unsubscribing you need to send them 3 to 4 emails that provide value. These emails should contain useful information, and then with every fourth or fifth email include your product recommendation. A proven strategy is to write a product review and then on the 4th or 5th email, send your list an email telling them about this great new product you've tried. In this email include the URL to this product review on your blog.

You will find that once the subscriber reads a few of your useful emails, they will begin to trust your product recommendations. Too many affiliate marketers spam their subscriber list with poorly written sales emails. So, ensure your emails are well written and your affiliate links or blog review links are clearly displayed.

Later in this book, I will show you how you how to cloak an affiliate link. Cloaking is a term to describe a method to disguise an affiliate link. A cloaked link will look like it is part of your website. The cloaked link will redirect the visitor from your blog to the vendors sales page. For each affiliate link you create I advise you to publish it in blue. Blue is regarded a safe color and more visitors will click a blue link. Furthermore, I always use blue words for my call to action.

Now that we have discussed a squeeze page, you now need to build an email subscriber list. There are many online applications available to build email lists such as Get Response and Mailchimp. The most popular email list building application is Aweber. Aweber costs 19 dollars per month and is worth every penny because of its simple to use functionality. The majority of successful internet marketers use Aweber.

Setting up Your Affiliate Blog

I previously covered why you should buy your own domain name and why should use Bluehost to host your blogs. In this chapter, I will discuss extra tips to deploy after setting up a Wordpress blog.

Cloak your affiliate link

A standard affiliate link looks ugly especially a Clickbank affiliate link. If you use a standard affiliate link, the visitor could think it's spammy and will not click it. Furthermore, a disguised affiliate link looks more professional and it will give your blog authority.

Let's discuss how to cloak an affiliate link using Pretty Link. Pretty Link is a Wordpress plugin. They offer a free lite version and a paid pro version. Forget the pro version, the lite version is adequate. To install the plugin, click plugins in the left menu on the Wordpress admin screen. Click Add New and type Pretty Link in the search bar. Find the Pretty Link plugin and install it, and then activate it. Pretty Link should now be displayed on the left side bar menu.

To set up a cloaked link, click on Add A Pretty Link and complete the fields. Remember to change the redirection field to 301 permanent. A 301 means the web page has moved permanently and is a search engine friendly way to redirect a web page.

When you set up your Pretty Link, you have the option to add a 'no follow' to the link. No follow will prevent a search engine from following and indexing your link. For search engine optimization it's always a good idea to make affiliate links no follow. Search engines tend to frown upon affiliate marketing websites.

Another option is to group your Pretty Link's

Grouping links is useful to track marketing campaigns. For example, you could keep all your YouTube links grouped in a folder for a specific product. Another Pretty Link feature is the ability to track the number of clicks for a link. This feature is used to track and analyze which Pretty Link receives the most clicks.

For example, you might want to include 2 or 3 links in a product review, so by naming each Pretty Link you create, you can then analyze and see which of the links receives the most clicks. This is useful since you might use different call-to-actions for each link and you can tell which call-to-action works best.

Tracking Your Performing Keyword and Phrases

It is important to know which of your keywords make you money when using PPC (Pay Per Click) advertising. With the right tools, tracking is simple and you will save a considerable amount of money using PPC. There are two activities you need to track and measure. You need to track the keywords which result in a click through, and the other is the keyword which people typed into the search engine that led to a purchase.

Finding out exactly how people purchased a Clickbank product is very important. Once you know which keywords are clicked and which keywords result in a sale, you will make money.

The most popular product to track clicks is Google Analytics. Google Analytics works by placing Javascript on web pages which you would like to track. The Javascript then captures a plethora of data and this data is displayed in the reporting section of Google Analytics.

My advice is to install Google Analytics on your website. However, if you choose to market a Clickbank product using PPC (Pay Per Click) advertising you could use the TID method of tracking.

The way to use the TID with PPC is to append a unique TID to each keyword and phrase in your PPC campaign. The only negative with this method is that it's time consuming if you are using over thirty plus keywords and phrases in your PPC campaign. It's time consuming because you would need to append thirty plus TID's.

Here's how to use the Clickbank TID method to track PPC keywords and phrases.

Before you begin you need to note all the TID's and keywords and phrases that you plan to use in your PPC campaign. Your spreadsheet would need three columns: Product Name, Keyword/Phrase and TID. For this example I'm using the Save My Marriage Today, Clickbank product. To keep this example simple, I'm going to use four phrases for my PPC campaign. They are - Save My Marriage, Stop Divorce, Marriage Tips and Marriage Advice. Next I need to create my TID's to append to my affiliate link.

Here's what my Clickbank affiliate link would like for the product Save My Marriage Today - http://50c8f5h3nc1o4rfdesfabkshdt.hop.clickbank.net/?tid=SMT1. At the end of this link you can see SMT1 as the appended TID. So SMT1 would represent my keyword phrase Save My Marriage. Now if I append SMT2 to the affiliate link, SMT2 would represent my keyword phrase Stop Divorce. The SMT3 would be Marriage Tips and SMT4 would be Marriage Advice.

My spreadsheet would like this:

Product Name	Keyword/Phrase	Clickbank TID
Save My Marriage Today	Save my marriage	SMT1

Save My Marriage Today	Stop divorce	SMT2
Save My Marriage Today	Marriage tips	SMT3
Save My Marriage Today	Marriage advice	SMT4

All you need to do now is add the affiliate link with the correct TID to the relevant keyword phrase in your PPC campaign.

To view the tracking results of these TID's you need to visit Clickbank's Analytics and click on the reporting section, then sort the data by Hops. The TID report will show important tracking data like hop count, and initial sales count. Using both data figures will help you decide which keywords were responsible for a sale. Furthermore, you can work out the conversion rate. The conversion rate is the sum of the hop count divided by initial sales count. The answers to this sum will let you know the average number of clicks needed to make a sale.

For example, if the TID hop count was 100 and you sold 5 products, the conversion rate would be 5%; you would need 20 clicks for every sale. Based on a 100 hop count - if you earned $30 per sale, 5 sales would earn you $150. If you spent 10 cents per click in your PPC campaign you're profit would be $140. Later in this book I discuss using PPC in more detail to promote Clickbank products.

The above PPC TID tracking example only works for direct linking. Direct linking is when the affiliate link is used in the PPC advert. When someone clicks your PPC advert, they are directed straight to the vendors sales page. As I previously mentioned in an earlier chapter, I prefer to send visitors to a product review page on my blog or to a product review video.

If you own a blog you can use Bevo Media or Prosper 202 to track profitable keywords and phrases. Prosper 202 is a self hosted application, which means you download and install the software on your server or the web hosts server. Therefore

Prosper 202 requires technical knowledge to install it. Bevo Media on the other hand is an online tracking application. Bevo Media is free and you can access it through any web browser.

I now use Bevo Media to track all my marketing campaigns. Occasionally I will use the direct linking method in a PPC campaign. I use direct linking to test new Clickbank products I promote. Once I know that this new product sells I will then spend time and create a marketing plan.

Bevo Media Affiliate Tracking

Bevo Media www.bevomedia.com is an online company who develop products to help affiliate marketers make money online. Their tracking platform offers excellent reporting and a simple way to track any product you promote online. Bevo Media offers tracking for PPC campaigns and landing page campaigns.

A landing page campaign is where you add their tracking code to your squeeze page blog page which contains affiliate links. Bevo Media charge a monthly subscription, but you can use their tracker for free by signing up for a free account.

To create a tracking link, you need to sign in and click Create New. The next page takes you to their wizard. All you need to do is follow the steps on this page to set up your tracking campaign. Bevo Media also offers fingerprint tracking.

Fingerprint tracking is an advanced way to track keywords phrases; unfortunately fingerprint tracking will not work with Clickbank TID's, therefore all your campaigns need to be created using Bevo Media's Manual Sub ID tracking method.

Fingerprint tracking requires Javascript to be added to the vendors page. The majority of vendors will not place this Javascript on their sales page; this is why I use the Manual Sub ID tracking method.

To install their Javascript tracking code on your blog, you will need some technical knowledge. Luckily there are help videos on how to add their tracking code; these videos can be found in the support section of their website. A feature that I like is that all the tracking data can be found on the Tracker tab. On the Tracker tab you can access reports such as number of clicks, which website the click originated from, the country where the click took place, the time of day of the click and other additional tracking information.

To see which keywords or phrases resulted in a Clickbank sale, you need to manually upload the TID which made the sale. Bevo Media will add a set of numbers to the Clickbank TID. All you need to do is upload this set of numbers. When you click on the Tracker tab, you can sort your results and identify which keyword or phrase was responsible for the sale.

To end this tracking chapter, I would like to introduce you to a cool free Clickbank app which I use on my iPhone. The app is called CB App. CB App is a simple way to track your sales and hop counts whilst on the go.

Six Methods to Promote a Clickbank Product

In this chapter I will share six ways to market and promote your Clickbank products. The following six methods do not involve link building or any search engine optimization. Since the latest set of Google algorithm updates, link building as a marketing strategy is no longer a good idea.

Affiliate marketers now need to think outside the box and use a variety of online marketing methods to drive visitors to their blog or squeeze page. If anyone or any book you read tells you to build back links to be a successful affiliate marketer, take it from me, they are wrong. Back link building is risky when you are trying to rank your website high in the search engine organic results.

The following six methods are by no means an exhausted list of ways to sell Clickbank products. My aim is to get a newbie started and hopefully the experienced Clickbank affiliate can learn a thing or two.

YouTube and Video Sharing Websites

To record a 3 to 5 minute product review video I use http://www.screencast-o-matic.com. This is an online video application that allows you record a video of your PC or Laptop screen and publish it straight on YouTube. In addition, you can download the video and publish it on video sharing sites such as https://vimeo.com.

My advice recording product review videos is to try and avoid recording PowerPoint presentations. The best way to record a review video is to film you talking about the product. If you are not confident to film yourself, then create a PowerPoint presentation, but do not substitute music with a voice over. You need to record your video with you talking in the background. A voice over video always outperforms music over videos when reviewing Clickbank products.

Remember not to make your video a sales pitch; make an informational based video. Use the exact method as I described in writing a review for a blog page. Use emotional words and clearly explain how the product will help the viewer. Sound sincere and show that you actually care about solving their problem.

Next optimize your video using the keyword phrases that you discovered with Traffic Travis so it appears in YouTube's search results. Alternatively use YouTube's suggested titles. To do this type the keyword or phrase in the search bar and see the titles YouTube suggests. Furthermore, use your keyword phrases to create tags for your video. Write a well written video description and include your unique Pretty Link at the top and bottom of the description. Finally add a link to your squeeze page with a call to action in your description.

Google Alerts and Blog Commenting

Google Alerts is a content notification service from Google. You can create alerts to notify you by email when new content is published online. The new content will match the words that you set up as an alert. I always set up alerts to get notified when blogs publish related content to my squeeze page. I then visit this blog post and post a comment which includes a link to my squeeze page. The objective here is to drive visitors to your squeeze and sign up on your email list. Email list building should be your number one strategy to focus on if you want to make a living promoting Clickbank products.

PPC – Pay per Click Advertising

What is pay per click advertising? PPC is paid advertising and is used to promote a website page or blog page. An affiliate marketer will use PPC to promote their review page or squeeze page or to directly link to the vendors sales page. PPC adverts are the boxes you see above and to the right in the organic search engine results. A PPC advert consists of a title description and a URL to persuade customers to click on the advert.

The two major PPC networks are Google Adwords and Bing Ads. I find that people who click PPC adverts are serious about solving their problems. This is known as targeted traffic.

The best PPC platform to promote Clickbank products is Bing Ads. The Bing Ads platform currently allows you to promote squeeze pages and affiliate marketing review pages. Bing will also allow you to link your PPC advert directly to the vendors sales page using your cloaked affiliate link or Bevo Media links. If you are a newbie affiliate marketer, I wouldn't jump in and begin using PPC.

PPC can be very expensive when you are inexperienced and will cost you money. The trick to using PPC is to learn the best converting keyword phrases. Once PPC is mastered, PPC is a great return on investment.

Planning a PPC Campaign

Before you open your wallet and spend money on PPC, you must have a clear idea on the keywords and phrases which convert into sales. Whilst you are discovering which keywords phrases convert into sales, you could buy a Bing Ads coupon. A coupon will add a credit to your Bing Ads account .You can find Bing Ads coupons on Fiverr.com. A coupon will let you try Bing Ads for free, until the coupon credit runs out.

When you know the conversion rate of your keyword phrases, you will be able to set the correct keyword bid amount in your Bing Ads account. The keyword bid is the money that you are willing to pay when someone clicks your ad.

Let's say the conversion rate for a Clickbank product is 5%. This means that for every 20 clicks you make a sale. If your keyword bid is 20 cents this means that you need to spend $4 to make a sale. If each sale earns you $30, you will make a profit of $26.

With a PPC campaign it's essential that you keep tracking and keep testing adverts and keywords to see which earns the most money.

Here are a few tips which I've learnt using PPC.

Add a video to your PPC landing page. I have found a video improves the keyword quality score. A higher quality score means your ad will be displayed more often and will lower your keyword bid price.

Improve your quality score by improving how relevant your site is to the bidded keyword.

Target the US and UK countries only. From my experience people who reside in the US and UK are more likely to purchase a Clickbank product.

Set a maximum daily budget so your budget does not spiral out of control!

Create multiple ad groups for each Clickbank product. For example, if you are promoting the "Save My Marriage Today" product, create a few ads for this product and create an ad group for each advert. Use keywords and phrases that are related to the groups advert.

If your landing page is a review of "Save My Marriage Today" then make this phrase your ads title. Then create keyword bids like "save my marriage today review" for this ad group. If someone is looking to buy "Save My Marriage Today", they will be more likely to click your advert and make a purchase.

Pay with a Tweet

In a world where social capital is king and everyone is scrambling for attention, Pay with a Tweet http://www.paywithatweet.com/ offers entrepreneurs, creative minds and established businesses a way to reach out to a media-saturated audience.

The concept behind Pay with a Tweet is simple. A single button is installed on your website, and when a browser clicks on it, they are given the chance to create a Tweet or a

Facebook post about your content. As soon as they have done so, they are granted access to a download that you provide.

At the most basic level, Pay with a Tweet offers your browsers and potential clients something concrete and valuable for something that they perceive as very simple. Essentially, all you are asking them to do is something that they would be doing anyway, just slightly modified for your needs. However, much like a single snowball can cause an avalanche, a single Tweet from one person can reach dozens of their friends who in turn continue the pattern.

Programs like Twitter and Facebook hold our social interactions together. They give us a face-to-face immediacy with friends, family and colleagues that we do not see every day, and the personal nature of these interactions lends them authority. As the content creator, you can reach a certain number of people with your own Tweets, but the number that your combined followers can reach by contacting their followers is exponentially greater!

One of the great benefits of Pay with a Tweet is that it relies on completely natural social patterns. You are not asking people to sell your product or to advertise it. Instead, you are only asking them to do something very simple, and you are rewarding them with something that they want.

How I Use Pay with a Tweet to Promote Clickbank Products

I write a short how to eBook in the same niche as the product and use this as a free giveaway. I create my product promotional affiliate link Tweet on Pay for a Tweet and copy the iFrame code for the button. I then set up a squeeze page on my blog and advertise the free eBook I created. I explain that the visitor can download this eBook if they click the Pay for a Tweet or Pay with a Facebook Post. They click the button, share my Tweet; boom, my Tweet goes viral. All I have to do is drive traffic to my squeeze page.

With more than 10,000 Pay with a Tweet buttons created and more than 400,000 files downloaded, the first social payment program has proven that it can get you the attention and the sales that you have been looking for!

Automated Social Media Marketing Bookmarking

If you know me or have read any of my books or articles on marketing, you will be familiar with my advocacy for Social Adr. If you can afford $19 per month, I recommend Social Adr - click here to sign up for an account at www.socialadr.com. You can cancel at anytime since it's a monthly subscription.

Social Adr is an automated online program which allows other users to share and post your message on their social media accounts. At this time a message can be posted on 30 high PR social media sites.

In brief Social Adr works by you creating a message with a link and the other users will then share your message across their social media accounts. You can bookmark multiple messages and your message will be fired out across the globe on autopilot.

Email List Building Using AWeber

I discussed email list building in a previous chapter. I cannot stress enough why list building is such a vital part of a successful Clickbank product marketing strategy. If you do not build a list, you are leaving money on the table. Simply put, list building is a method where you capture prospects details, and then carefully build a relationship, and turn these prospects into loyal customers. To encourage visitors to sign up to your list, you will offer them a free gift.

The key is not to spam them, and the ultimate objective is to gain their trust and build relationships. From experience the best way to approach list building is to deploy a 4 to 1 formula. You need to email to your list 4 emails that only contain useful content and the 5th email should be a promotional or sales based email. If you send your list too many sales focused emails in succession, you will for sure lose the trust of the people on your list and they will unsubscribe.

Another tip is not to send your list emails on a daily or weekly basis. I therefore recommend only sending an email every 10-14 days, in addition mixing up the frequency and leaving 30 days between some emails works well.

There are a number of free and paid for online applications to build a subscriber list. By far the most popular is www.aweber.com because it's simple to use and has offers some great features.

[Click here to sign up for an AWeber account. The first month costs $1.](#)

Closing Thoughts

Remember to test and track all your affiliate marketing efforts, record your findings in a spreadsheet and analyze why a particular campaign worked.

I would like to say thank you for choosing my book since there are a large number of similar Kindle books. Would you be so kind to tell your friends, family and work colleagues about my book?

Please would you take a few moments and leave a few positive words on Amazon. After all, you should be able to easily make 1000 times the $3 that you spent on this book. Positive feedback will help future readers find my book and will help me to sell more books. And don't forget to grab your free gift, my 5,000 word Twitter Marketing Guide.

Here's the download link.

http://www.darrenackers.com/free-twitter-marketing-guide

If you would like to connect, please do so using the following and let me know you bought my book:

Blog http://www.darrenackers.com/

Twitter https://twitter.com/darren_ackers

LinkedIn https://uk.linkedin.com/in/darrenackers

In addition, if you need any help, advice, or feel I missed something in this book, please do email me admin@darrenackers.com - I would love to hear from you.

The very best of luck

Darren

www.ingramcontent.com/pod-product-compliance
Lightning Source LLC
Chambersburg PA
CBHW070918180526
45168CB00005B/2060